How to Be a Spy

Illustrated by Mathias Sielfeld
Written by Daniel Nesquens

Translation from Spanish by Little Gestalten

Font: *Archer Pro* by Tobias Frere-Jones and
Jonathan Hoefler, *Adobe Garamond* by Robert
Slimbach, *Beloved* by Laura Worthington,
Bernhard Gothic by URW Type Foundry, *Brown
Pro* by Nick Shinn, *Neuzon* and *Chainprinter*
by Ray Larabie, *Citadel* by Tobias Frere-Jones,
Condor by David Jonathan Ross, *LTC Pabst
Oldstyle* by Frederic W. Goudy and Paul D. Hunt

Printed by Wilco Art Books Amersfoort,
Netherlands
Made in Europe

Published by Little Gestalten, Berlin 2022
ISBN 978-3-96704-737-0

The Spanish original edition
Manual para espías was published by
Editorial Flamboyant S.L.

www.editorialflamboyant.com

© Editorial Flamboyant S.L., 2022
© Text: Daniel Nesquens, 2021
© Illustrations: Mathias Sielfeld, 2021

© for the English edition:
Little Gestalten, an imprint of
Die Gestalten Verlag GmbH&Co.KG,
Berlin 2022.

For more information, and to order books, please visit
www.little.gestalten.com.

Bibliographic information published by the Deutsche
Nationalbibliothek.

The Deutsche Nationalbibliothek lists this publication in
the Deutsche Nationalbibliografie; detailed bibliographic
data are available online at www.dnb.de.

MIX
Paper from
responsible sources
FSC® C004472

This book was printed on
paper certified according to
the standards of the FSC®.

HOW TO BE A SPY

Daniel Nesquens · Oyemathias

LITTLE GESTALTEN

CONTENTS

"IF SOMEONE SAYS HE PROVIDED ME
WITH SECRET INFORMATION, THE CRIME
WAS COMMITTED BY HIM, NOT BY ME."

Margaretha Geertruida Zelle,
a.k.a. Mata Hari, dancer and double agent

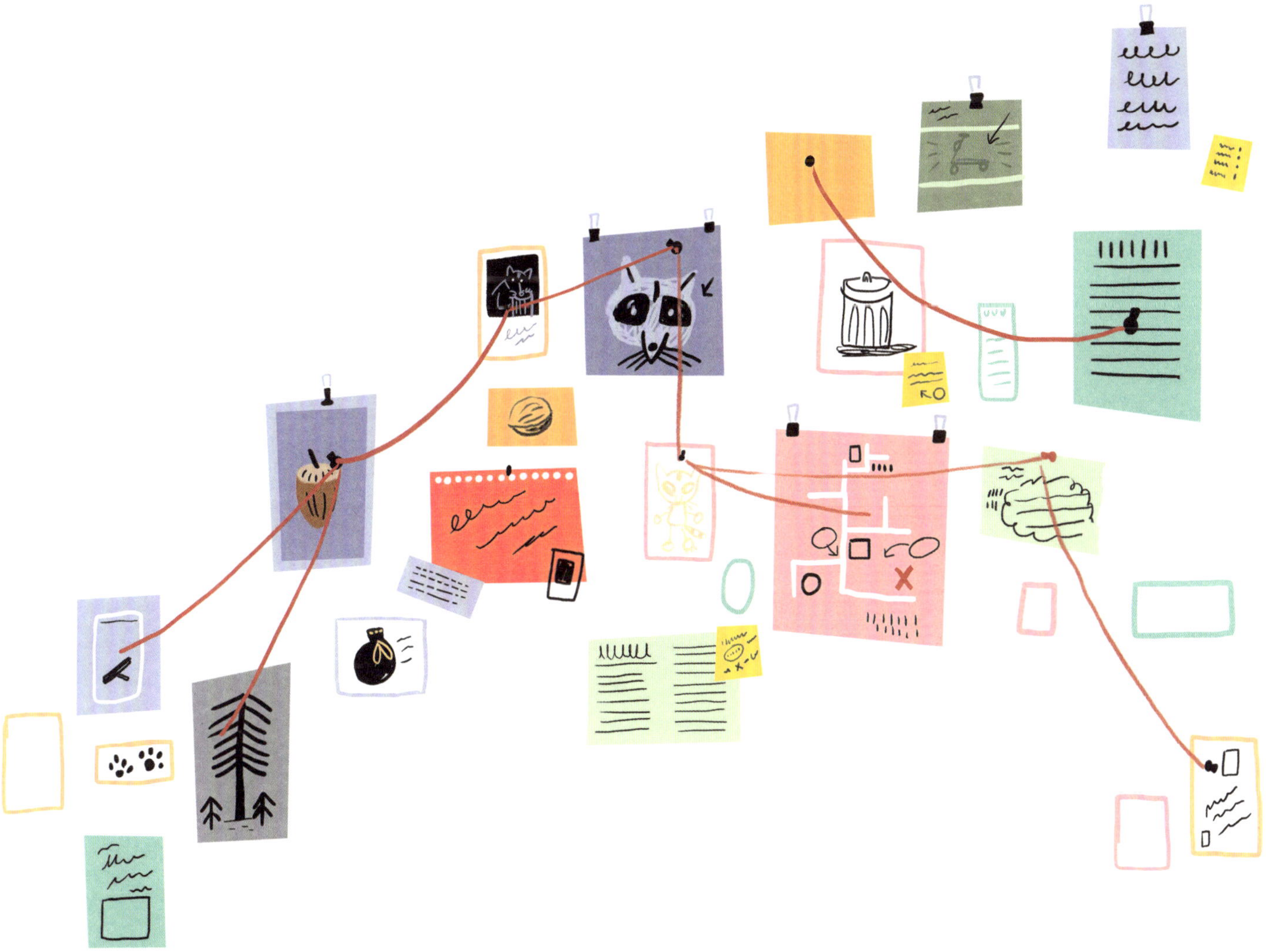

WHAT IS A SPY?

The meaning of the term *spy* comes from the Italian word *spiare*, which can be translated as "to look out".

If espionage is the art of analyzing and observing the opponent, we can define a spy as a person who, on request, is dedicated to obtaining secret information in different ways, almost all of them risky and dangerous. Because of this, spies are daring, astute, courageous, and, well...nosy! But they must also be solitary, discreet, reserved, attentive, polite, and elegant. Spies provide data and let their employers analyze it. Their work can be exciting, dangerous, and very challenging.

TOP SECRET

To be a spy you don't have to wear a trench coat, have an elegant mustache, or know how to get around Vienna. You don't have to practise magic tricks, carry a buffalo skin briefcase, or speak a hundred languages...It is enough to be an ordinary person (with great instincts) who is willing to do an extraordinary job. If you meet these conditions, you have much to gain, but if you like to talk too much or give too many details of your private life...then maybe it is not the job for you.

PAY ATTENTION TO EVERYTHING YOU READ. DON'T GET DISTRACTED.

DON'T MISS A SINGLE THING.

THE RESUME OF A GOOD SPY

The recruitment process for a secret agent can take months, with many tests and many hours of interviews—including hours of interrogations regarding one's personal life.

Aptitude, talent, confidence, security, discretion...

Not everyone can be a good spy. There are bound to be situations that can make you freeze. Some of these situations must be overcome in a fraction of a second—and they have to be taken care of well, and without anyone noticing.

According to studies by European neuroscientists, the brain of a spy is "just a smidgen" different from that of other human beings. And it is not that they have two cerebellums, or that the frontal lobe is pistachio green, no. But it is indisputable that a good spy's brain is "just a little bit" different from that of other human beings. A good spy has an agile, dynamic mind. Apparently, the speed of the electrical signals that reach their brains is faster, as if they were in a hurry. Quick!

BESIDES BEING PERCEPTIVE, THERE ARE OTHER IMPORTANT SKILLS THAT A GOOD SPY MUST HAVE.
TAKE NOTE:

DISCRETION: a spy knows that certain types of information must be kept secret.

EXTENSIVE KNOWLEDGE AND MASTERY OF NEW TECHNOLOGIES: nowadays, it would be impossible to perform this job without the necessary proficiency in these technological skills.

EXCELLENT PHYSICAL FITNESS: you don't need to run a hundred meter sprint in less than 12 seconds, but you do need to train speed, endurance, flexibility, and power.

HIGH INTELLECTUAL CAPACITY: logical thinking helps a lot.

GOOD PRESENCE: a spy who dresses like a clown would never blend in!

AND SOME OTHER SKILLS:

- The ability to work with others in a team.
- Quick thinking and problem-solving skills.
- Keeping cool under pressure.
- A wide range of social skills: empathy, listening skills, respect, credibility, patience, courtesy . . .

- Language skills. If possible, many.
- And a sense of humor. This does not mean that you need to know hundreds of jokes, but a good laugh makes us better inside and out!
— What do you call a fake noodle?
— An im-pasta

TYPES OF SPIES

The famous general, military strategist, and philosopher of ancient China, Sun Tzu, wrote *The Art of War* around the year 512 BCE As a result of his own experience, he determined in his book that there were five types of spy: the Local, the Insider, the Double Agent, the Floater, and the Liquidable.

THE LOCAL

The spy hired from among the people of a certain population.

THE INSIDER

This one works among the enemy officials.

"INFORMATION CANNOT BE OBTAINED FROM GHOSTS OR SPIRITS. IT MUST BE OBTAINED FROM PEOPLE WHO KNOW THE ADVERSARY'S SITUATION."
– SUN TZU

THE FLOATER

They are responsible for transmitting reports.

THE DOUBLE AGENT

The one hired among the enemy spies—pushing them to collaborate with the side they were originally commissioned to spy on.

THE LIQUIDABLE

This is the spy who must contaminate the enemy's information with all kinds of false data and reports.

GOLDEN RULES OF BEING A GOOD SPY

There are more than a dozen rules—each of these are very important...

EYES OPEN!
Pay attention and watch everything.

BE PATIENT AND DISCIPLINED

TRUST YOUR INSTINCTS!
Pay attention to your gut feelings.

DON'T depend on **TECHNOLOGY.**

BE STRONG!
Float like a butterfly, sting like a bee.

DON'T STICK TO YOUR OWN HABITS:
Be weary of doing things without thinking.

DON'T TAKE ANYTHING FOR GRANTED.

Be a **WELL INFORMED PERSON.**
You must be up to date on the latest news.

BE CAREFUL, PRUDENT, ASTUTE, IMAGINATIVE...
A setback does not mean that you have to abandon your work. You must make quick decisions in urgent moments and different scenarios.

KNOW YOUR ADVERSARY—
study them in all fields.

Secure the
**ELEMENT
OF SURPRISE**
against the enemy.

**DO NOT
TAKE RISKS**
or go beyond
the call of duty.

And a bonus golden rule from Ian Fleming, the creator of James Bond.
Never forget:

"ONCE IS A HAPPENSTANCE. TWICE IS A COINCIDENCE. THREE TIMES IS ENEMY ACTION."

THE REAL JAMES BOND?

Ian Fleming and double (possibly even triple) agent "Dusko" Popov met in 1941 in a hotel in Estoril, Portugal. Fleming was very impressed by this cultured, refined, polyglot man—so much so that he was part of the inspiration behind the character of James Bond.

CHOOSE THE TIME,
the occasion, and the place to perform your maneuvers.

USE CLEAR AND CONCISE
writing in your reports. Don't include any unnecessary information.

SPY TECHNIQUES

For thousands of years, the most up-to-date, incredible, and fabulous espionage techniques and strategies you can imagine have been used all over the world.

In the 21st century, the spy's modus operandi (the way they work) has evolved due to the technological boom, but since the world began, spies have developed the most ingenious and surprising methods to carry out their risky operations.

SURVEILLANCE IS AN ORGANIZED AND PLANNED OPERATION TO OBSERVE SOMETHING OR SOMEONE.

FACE-TO-FACE SURVEILLANCE

In order to carry out good surveillance, a precise study of the area, its possible routes, and the movements of the target must be carried out. It is advisable to have detailed maps available, as well as a reconnaissance of the area to detect the most appropriate surveillance points: kiosks, cafés with large windows, stores, parks, buildings with rooftops…

And of course—never be seen!

REMOTE SURVEILLANCE

Surveillance is not only the monitoring of a person's movements. It can also be done at a distance using listening devices. Technological advances have evolved tremendously over the years: mini-cameras with remote connections and artificial intelligence to recognize people, night vision devices, the latest generation of microphones hidden in the most unsuspecting objects that transmit audio in high quality…

ANTENNA

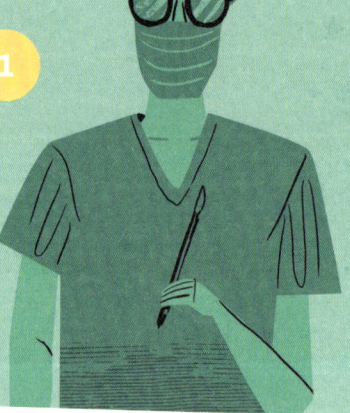

1

OPERATION ACOUSTIC KITTY

BATTERY

TRANSMITTER

MICROPHONE

A very unique example of remote spying involved surgically implanting a microphone, an antenna, a transmitter, and a battery in a trained cat! The trick was to get everything inserted in such a way that the animal would not act strangely. The CIA considered the operation a high-risk experiment. And rightly so.

1 Make sure the cat has everything it needs: battery, microphone, tail, ears…

2 Clear path, tail up, and hopefully no rodents…

3 Maximum precision! Agents to delete unnecessary conversations immediately.

4 Any eagles around? They can put your entire operation at risk…

INFILTRATION

Infiltration is a method of espionage where you introduce your own spies into other organisations specifically to collect the most useful information from the enemy so that you can get ahead of their plans.

This maneuver consists of using an undercover agent (sometimes known as a "mole"), whose task is to gain the trust of the people who have the most compromising information and then pass it on to your side.

Types of infiltrator

1

A person with extensive training who infiltrates the adversary as a native.

Spy Eli Cohen posed as a very patriotic businessman and even befriended the president of Syria!

2

A member of the enemy country posing as someone originally from a friendly third country.

PENETRATION

Although it may seem the same as infiltration, it is not. Penetration is based on collaboration with an individual on the enemy side to obtain precise information about a clear target. The penetration agent voluntarily presents themselves as a deserter, or even as a traitor. They may even claim to have important information that can dazzle their new friends! With this ruse, they can obtain first-hand information and data that they can then transfer back to their country of origin.

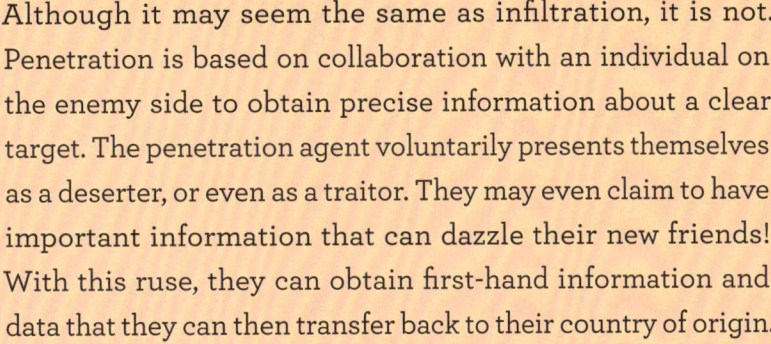

3

A spy who is already working with the enemy.

Mata Hari (agent H-21) was recruited by the German intelligence service when she was working as a dancer in a music hall in Berlin. Her mission was to obtain military information in France. But when she arrived in France, she offered to work as a spy for the French secret service. A true double agent.

4

The agent who shows up unexpectedly offering their services to the adversary.

METHODS OF COMMUNICATION

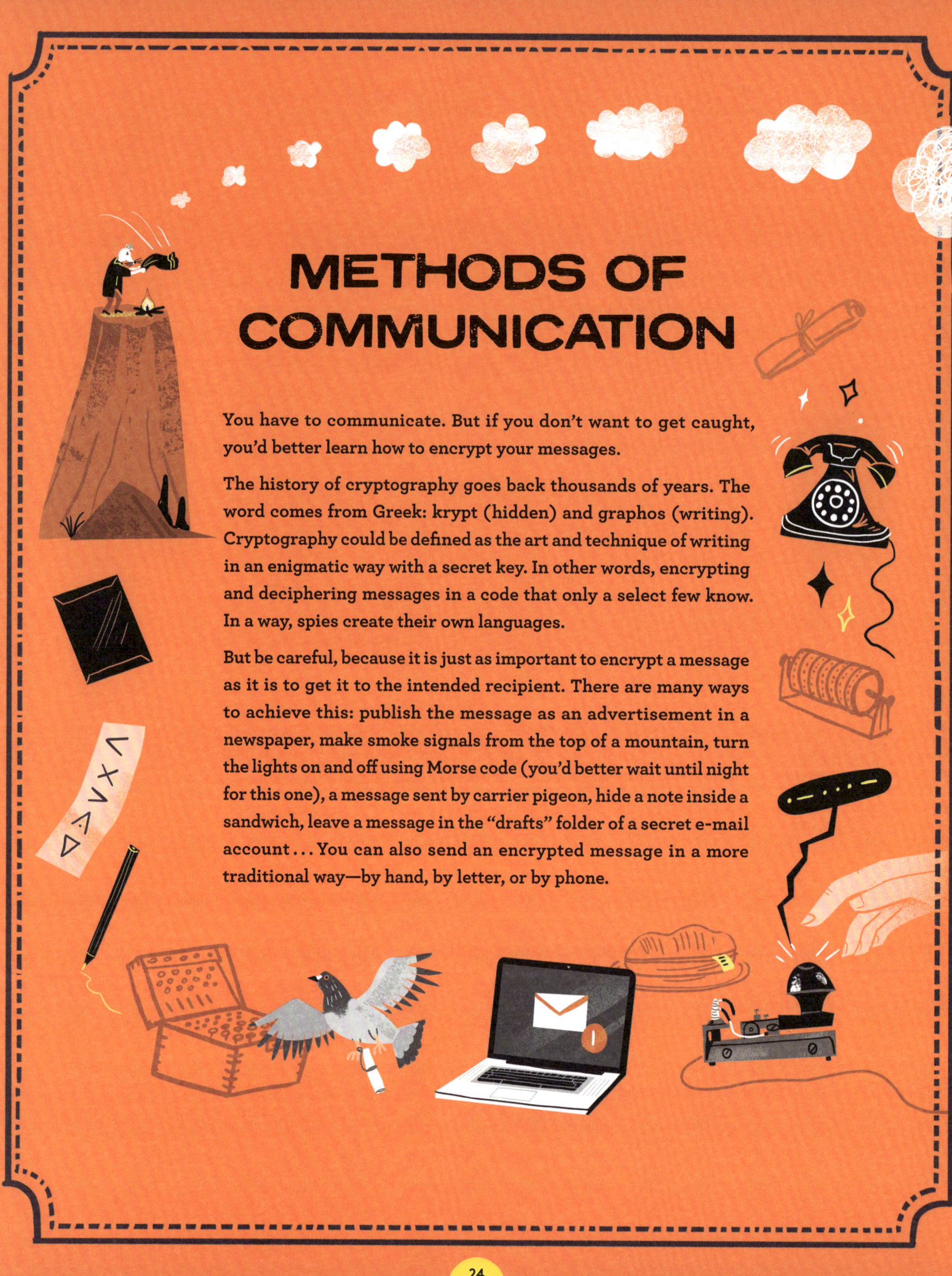

You have to communicate. But if you don't want to get caught, you'd better learn how to encrypt your messages.

The history of cryptography goes back thousands of years. The word comes from Greek: krypt (hidden) and graphos (writing). Cryptography could be defined as the art and technique of writing in an enigmatic way with a secret key. In other words, encrypting and deciphering messages in a code that only a select few know. In a way, spies create their own languages.

But be careful, because it is just as important to encrypt a message as it is to get it to the intended recipient. There are many ways to achieve this: publish the message as an advertisement in a newspaper, make smoke signals from the top of a mountain, turn the lights on and off using Morse code (you'd better wait until night for this one), a message sent by carrier pigeon, hide a note inside a sandwich, leave a message in the "drafts" folder of a secret e-mail account... You can also send an encrypted message in a more traditional way—by hand, by letter, or by phone.

Historically, cryptography has always been linked to state secrets and major wars. Today, it is responsible for the study and application of algorithms and systems to bring security to information and communication.

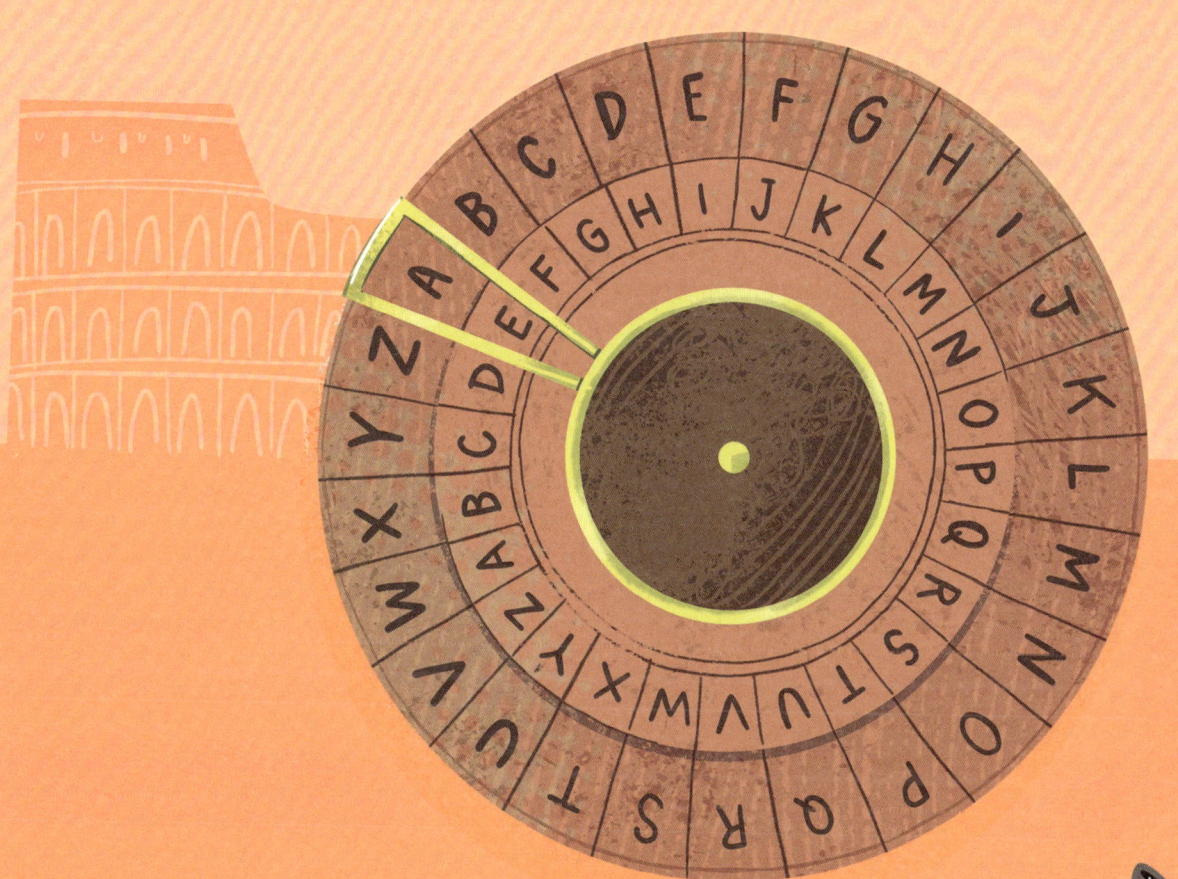

XVC WIRHMRK E QIWWEKI XS E JVMIRH YWMRK XLMW GSHI!

TRY SENDING A MESSAGE TO A FRIEND USING THIS CODE!

THE ALBERTI CIPHER

In 1466, the painter and architect Leon Batista Alberti invented what became known as the "Alberti cipher." It is considered one of the first polyalphabetic ciphers created by humans.

It consists of two concentric copper discs on which the alphabet is engraved. The two discs rotate independently and are used to encrypt and decrypt messages.

MORSE CODE

During World War I, the Germans used Dutch windmills to communicate. Taking advantage of the movement of the blades, they sent messages in Morse code.

JEFFERSON'S RECORDS

The third president of the United States devised an encryption system that used a cylinder with a set of 36 wheels or discs. Each disc contained the 26 letters of the English alphabet distributed around the rim, so that by turning them, a message could be composed on any of their lines. Then, any other line of the cylinder was selected, the message was copied in code and sent.

To decipher the note, the receiver had to place the letters of the code they had received in the correct order on their own cylinder and locate the line of letters with the message in order to see their true meaning. Yes, this seems very complicated—see the illustration below for help, my spy friend.

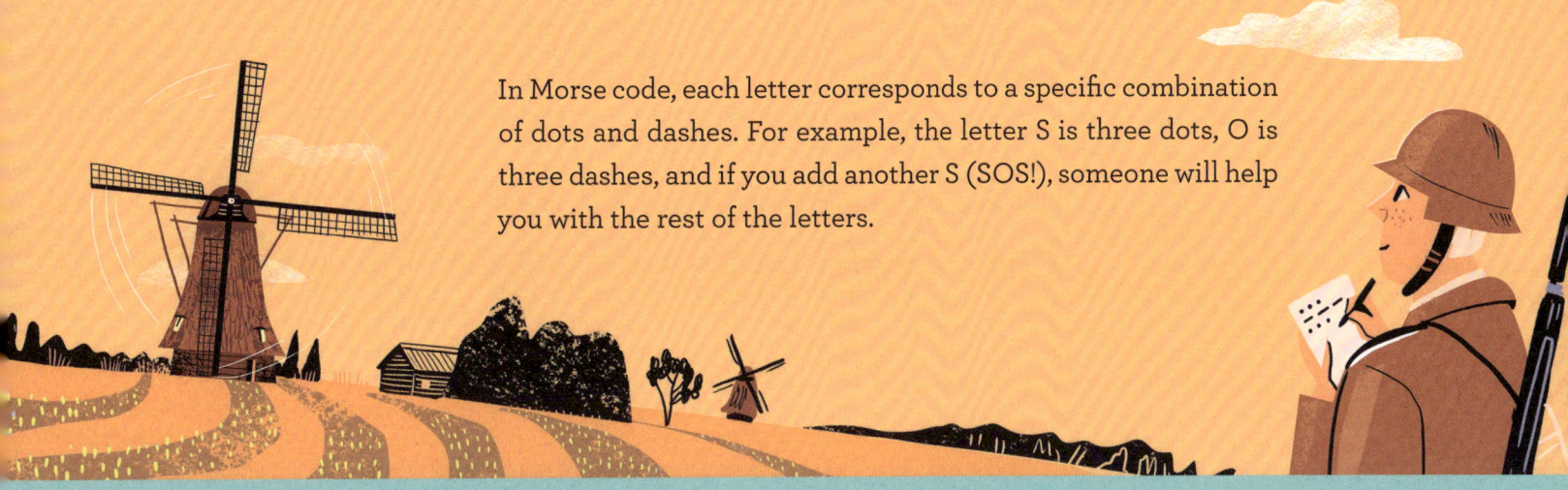

In Morse code, each letter corresponds to a specific combination of dots and dashes. For example, the letter S is three dots, O is three dashes, and if you add another S (SOS!), someone will help you with the rest of the letters.

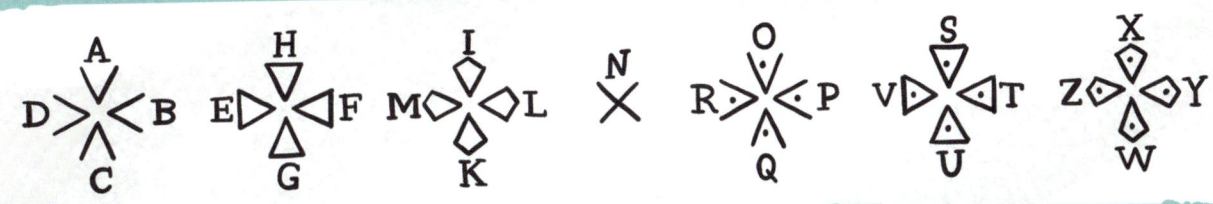

THE FREEMASON CIPHER

The Freemason cipher is a simple substitution cipher that exchanges letters for symbols set out in a diagram. It is also known as the Rosicrucian cipher, since its creation is attributed to an esoteric religious group or secret society of medieval Germany with that name.

THE ENIGMA MACHINE

The Enigma machine was patented in 1918 by Arthur Scherbius, an expert electro-mechanical engineer from Germany who died unaware of the dramatic influence his invention had on the development of World War II.

At that time, the famous and complex Enigma machine was adopted by the Germans to encrypt and decrypt messages. German submarines stationed in the Atlantic used it to communicate by radio with each other and with their country without any difficulty.

The Enigma machine resembled a typewriter and was made up of both electrical and mechanical parts, including a series of keys that were actually switches. When pressed, they moved rotating cylinders that would substitute one letter for another.

Although the operation seemed simple, as a system of encrypted messaging it was priceless, since the number of possible combinations was very, very high. Almost one hundred and sixty trillion!

Eventually, the German messages were deciphered. The capture of the German submarine U-110 gave the British navy one of these Enigma machines which was then taken to Bletchley Park in England.

Here, Alan Turing (considered the father of computer science) worked with the codebreakers to discover the key to the secret language of the Enigma.

Although it is estimated that more than eight thousand women worked at Bletchley Park (in 1945 they made up 75 % of the staff!), the important role played by mathematician and cryptanalyst Joan Clarke stands out.

She worked side by side with Turing and his team to unravel the workings of this message coding system, thus contributing to the end of World War II.

DEAD DROP

Sometimes also called a dead letterbox...

This is an old-school technique for secretly passing information or packages and avoiding being there when the other person picks up the information.

1 Establish the delivery location
2 Check all around you—go unnoticed
3 Leave the information at the drop
4 Your contact will pick it up from the drop
5 Leave without being noticed

Spy Robert Hanssen, a former U.S. FBI agent who spied for the Soviet Union (and later post-communist Russia) for more than 20 years, was arrested in February 2001 in a Virginia park as he was about to deposit a package containing important documents in a dead letterbox and pick up a good deal of money in another one.

MISTAKES A SPY SHOULD NOT MAKE

Being a spy has its complications, believe me. It's not as easy as you might think. First of all, you have to deny that you are one, no matter how much you are asked. If a spy says they're a spy, they've already messed up!

Veteran British spy Kim Philby's favorite phrase was, "Deny, deny, and deny."

Are you a spy?

No.

Are you sure you're not a spy?

No.

How about a Secret Agent?

No.

So you deny it?

I deny being a spy, a secret agent, and a Manchester City supporter.

And that briefcase with the secret documents?

This is just a revolutionary formula for a hair growth serum.

You might want to buy a couple of liters...

4

Here are some helpful warnings and tips so that you never make these mistakes:

1. Be sure you have the necessary and appropriate equipment for each occasion. Ignorance of your conditions can be very dangerous.

2. Never leave a trace. Any record of your work must be erased, both in person and technologically.

3. There are situations that require patience and calm. Signs of anxiety (trembling, nausea, sweating…) can give us away. And never lose your temper!

4. Don't get caught in the act of monitoring (discreet surveillance from a distance).

5. Don't let your bad memory cause trouble—don't leave a dossier with compromising photos or a USB memory stick on the bus!

There are more things that could cause you problems as a spy . . .

1. Believing you're a movie character.

2. Excessive nose-picking.

3. Wearing flashy clothes.

4. Spending too much money.

5. Being arrogant.

6. Neglecting your daily grooming—especially your dental hygiene.

7. Not knowing how to set your alarm clock.

8. Confusing east with west, or Switzerland with Sweden.

9. Getting distracted.

Werner Von Janowski (aka Bobby) is often considered the worst spy in history. Apparently nothing ever went right for him.

WHAT TO PUT IN YOUR SPY BAG

JUST IN CASE...

CG 5824-S, known as Morris Childs, was an FBI agent infiltrating the Communist Party of the United States. He was born Moishe Chilovski in 1902 to a Jewish family in what was still the Russian Empire. He lived his early years in Russia until his father, an active opponent of the regime of Tsar Nicholas II, managed to escape to the United States.

Morris Childs was nothing like a movie spy: he was very discreet, very normal looking. His regular appearance was his best defense. A single false move could give him away, so he acted with extreme caution. Maybe that's why he always filled his suitcase with countless strange things. "Just in case," he would answer when asked why. "Just in case." This would eventually become his nickname.

Here is a long list of "other things" for your spy suitcase:

A water bottle, a corkscrew, a pencil, a wooden clothespin, a spare phone, a bar of soap, cough drops, an eraser, a rubber band, a visor cap, a dictionary, a toaster (just in case), a bow tie, a toiletry kit, a chocolate bar, a box cutter, a folding umbrella, a sponge, a comb, mosquito repellent, hand cream, vegetable soup (just in case), flip-flops, headphones, a book, a thin blanket, a padlock, a can of squid in its ink…

STATUS: ACTIVE DUTY

Congratulations! After reading this book, you can almost say you're a secret agent. You already know a lot about how this special world works—so now it's time to take action.

CREATE YOUR SECRET IDENTITY

It's important to choose a good code name so that no one knows who you really are. Make up a life different from the one you have. Don't make it too extreme— it's easier to remember simple things. If you tell too many tales, you will have trouble remembering the details and you may embarrass yourself!

SECRET ID

MARIACHI SQUIRREL

IT DOESN'T HURT TO GET A PROFESSIONAL ID CARD, BUT YOU SHOULD NEVER CARRY IT WITH YOU, IN CASE YOU ARE CAPTURED BY THE ENEMY!

This ID will self destruct in 3, 2, 1...

BOOM!

Remember that spies have excellent taste in clothing. It is not necessary to dress up in a suit and tie or an evening gown, but under no circumstances should you wear a tattered T-shirt or some felt slippers. You know, the kind you wear around the house? Unless the mission requires it, of course.

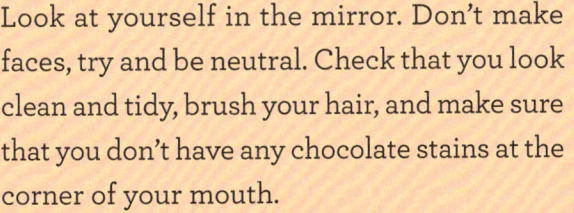

Look at yourself in the mirror. Don't make faces, try and be neutral. Check that you look clean and tidy, brush your hair, and make sure that you don't have any chocolate stains at the corner of your mouth.

Make a list of your skills. Not all spies are good at everything and not all are good at doing the same job: Mata Hari was a great dancer and Joan Clarke was brilliant at mathematics, and both were legendary agents. There is a mission for every type of spy.

TOP SECRET
(Secret file)

MACADAMIA TREE AGENCY

NAME: ARDY KOEM

CODE NAME: MARIACHI SQUIRREL

IN CASE OF AN EMERGENCY, CALL:
MY TWIN BROTHER, KALVIM BELOMYS

VEHICLES HE CONTROLS: ALL

SPECIALITIES: MOST DIFFICULT SITUATIONS

LANGUAGES SPOKEN: AT LEAST TEN

SECRET MEETING PLACE:
SIXTH BRANCH OF THE COMMON WALNUT
TREE, BLACKTHORN STREET

SECRET PASSPHRASE:
THE PANDA ATE ALL MY ICE CREAM

**The name of your mission
is also important.**
Something like Operation Origami
or Chipmunk Galaxy Mission...

PLAN YOUR SURVEILLANCE

Make your plan of action beforehand. A good spy never leaves anything to chance! Study maps of the area, locate in advance the places where you could hide or go unnoticed, and ALWAYS have a safe escape route.

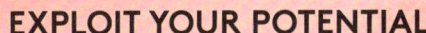

EXPLOIT YOUR POTENTIAL

Richebourg was a dwarf and a French spy. He was 58 centimeters tall and was very intelligent with a great memory. He smuggled messages in and out of Paris while disguised as a baby in a carriage.

Study your target: analyze their schedule, observe their movements, note down their routines—every detail can be important.

ENCRYPT YOUR MESSAGES

Is a simple message a good enough reason to get caught?

Think about how you're going to encode your messages.
Here are some ideas (more on pages 25–27):

A

Tidy up the letters in your message with the transposition method.

1 First, compose your message.

THE BEAVER DANCES ONLY AT DAWN EXCEPT TODAY

```
 1   2   3
 T   H   E
 B   E   A
 V   E   R
 D   A   N
 C   E   S
 O   N   L
 Y   A   T
 D   E   W
 N   E   X
 C   T   P
 T   A   O
 D       Y
```

2 Write each letter of your message in a column, in order. Let's say you make three columns (1, 2, 3).

3 Cut out the columns and mix them up (2, 1, 3).

```
 2   1   3
 H   T   E
 E   B   A
 E   V   R
 A   D   N
 E   C   S
 N   O   L
 A   Y   T
 A   D   W
 E   N   X
 E   C   P
 T   T   O
 A   D   Y
```

4 Copy out the resulting letters as though they were a message that made complete sense.

HTEEBAEVVRADNECSNOLAYTADWENXECPTTOADY

B

Use a substitution system. Change the language setting of your computer keyboard. With the Greek keyboard, your **Q** key, for example, would be the: symbol! Anyone who doesn't know that you have used this trick will understand nothing.

Be sure to remember how to return to your original language, or your computer will no longer be of any use to you...

C /// Go back to the classics and make a Spartan scytale (one of the first known secret codes!). All you need is a stick, a strip of cloth, and a pen!

1 Twist the strip of cloth onto the stick.

2 Write the message vertically. This way it can only be read if it is threaded onto a stick of the same thickness as the one that was used to write it.

HEY THERE

3 Hide the message—the Spartans would use these scytales as a belt!

EQUIP YOURSELF WITH THE ESSENTIALS

The Art of Persuasion

The art of persuasion is one of the most valued skills for a spy.
Try to obtain information without arousing suspicion.

Here are some tips:

- Avoid pretentious language. Speaking to others in a pompous manner can put you on the spot!

- Turn questions into statements. Questions into statements? Yes, questions into statements.

- Ask very specific questions.

- Play the game of misdirection—distract them. Did you know there is a fountain pen that writes with pure cocoa ink?

- Act as a double agent and establish a trusting relationship with your target or people around them. Collect evidence, analyze the facts, and discreetly interview everyone.

- Be friendly but natural! Use your charm, use common sense, and put all your skills to use.

- The appearance of normality is your best weapon. Be bold, patient, and calm. Use small movements to make sure everything seems under control.

And always rememeber:
S-D-C
Stealthy, Discreet, Calculating

WHAT IF YOU GET CAUGHT?

Haven't you read page 32? "Deny, deny, and deny". That's your only way out. Act indifferent, with feigned naturalness—you have to deny everything they throw in your face. And if they still don't believe it, here are some phrases to disprove those compromising statements…

If the evidence they have against you is very, very strong, you can always say that you were "researching" for a school project!

Perhaps a school assignment on…the consequences of…chocolates on…the nervous system?

Before you get to this point, you still have time to find out if your suspicions are unfounded (or if you are right…), therefore you can still use this information to your advantage and leave some false clues…or simply run away!

THE DROP OF GLUE

Oleg Gordievski, a KGB double agent, was sent to Copenhagen with his wife to gather information and recruit potential agents: in other words, to spy. The Danish security service soon realized that Gordievski (known there as Uncle Gormsson) was a KGB spy. Taking advantage of the fact that the couple had been invited to a dinner party, they installed microphones inside their home. But Gordievski had a bad feeling about this invitation and, just in case, left a drop of glue between the living room door and the frame.

When he returned from dinner, the invisible seal had been broken. Then he knew: he was being watched.

HISTORICAL CURIOSITIES

NEOLITHIC

(What times those were!)
There is some evidence of
surprise attacks on their enemies
that, according to scholars,
had very specific purposes.

SARGON I OF AKKAD

In the 3rd millennium BCE
he created a network of
spies and became the first
emperor in history.

ORIGIN OF ENCRYPTED MESSAGES

In Ancient Greece they knew
that if it was important to obtain
information from the enemy, it
was equally important to transmit
orders in a secure way.

ROMAN EMPIRE

All politicians had
their network of spies.
According to historians,
General Publius Cornelius
Scipio Africanus sent
centurions disguised as
enslaved people into the
enemy camp. This way,
he obtained valuable
information and managed
to defeat the Carthaginian
general Hannibal.

THE POCHTECA: TRADERS AND SPIES

These Aztec traders used their constant travels selling all kinds of goods to obtain information from the peoples they later conquered.

AMBASSADOR OR SECRET AGENT?

In the Middle Ages, the role of agents (almost always ambassadors) became widespread in the imperial courts. They spoke to merchants, doctors, sailors, and more to obtain valuable and precise information.

CARDINAL RICHELIEU

During the reign of Louis XIII appears the figure of Cardinal and Prime Minister Richelieu (you'll recognize him if you read *The Three Musketeers*…), who is considered the inventor of domestic espionage.

THE SHINOBIS

In Imperial Japan,
the shinobi appear.
That is, the real
ninjas. These were
Samurai who were
commissioned by the
government to carry
out espionage work.

NAPOLEON I

He organized a
modern and efficient
espionage service
and secret police.

DOMINGO FRANCISCO
JORGE BADÍA Y LEBLICH

The King of Spain, Charles IV, had
this adventurer pose as an exiled
Arab prince using the name
Ali Bey-Abbassi and—as one of the
most audacious and adventurous
agents in history—attempt to overthrow
the Sultan of Morocco!

CULPER RING

The network of spies created
by George Washington
and Benjamin Tallmadge
during the American
War of Independence
between American colonists
and the British army.

INDUSTRIAL ESPIONAGE

John Lombe was the son of a silk spinner and merchant who had a factory in Derby, England, in the 18th century. Knowing that the best silk thread was being woven in Piedmont, Italy, he traveled there with the purpose of learning about this innovative mechanized production. He would sneak into the Italian factory at night and, thanks to his skills as a draughtsman he would trace the machines. Back in Derby, he reproduced all his discoveries.

WOMEN SPY TOO

By 1914, when World War I broke out in Europe, the network of spies had increased dramatically, with a special focus on the female role. A good number of women acted in this role—both in the field and behind the scenes. The legendary Mata Hari; Maria Bochkariova, the leader of the Russian soldiers; Dorothy Lawrence, the journalist who disguised herself as a soldier; the English nurse Edith Cavell; the Nobel Prize winner Marie Curie herself! These, among others, were pioneers of this new promotion of agents.

20TH-21ST CENTURY

OPERATION BARBAROSSA

Richard Sorge (1895–1944) was a Soviet secret service agent. He founded a perfect international espionage network and his reports not only saved Moscow, but also contributed significantly to the victory over the Nazis.

Sorge reported the exact date of the Nazi attack on the USSR, which became known as "Operation Barbarossa", but Stalin ignored the message.

He was discovered, sentenced to death, and executed by hanging on November 7, 1944, on the anniversary of the Bolshevik revolution in Russia.

MANHATTAN
Project

Margarita Konionkova (1895–1980), was a Soviet spy on U.S. territory whose mission was focused on research and development of the first nuclear weapons, known as the "Manhattan Project".

Sergey Konyonov, an artist and Margarita's husband, was commissioned to create a bust of Albert Einstein. It was then that the supposedly accidental relationship between the brilliant spy and the author of the theory of relativity began. Their romance was confirmed in the form of letters they regularly wrote to each other.

A brilliant cryptanalyst

Elisabeth Smith Friedman (1892–1980), born in a small town in Indiana, was one of the first cryptanalysts. She was a literature teacher and thanks to her knowledge of Latin and Greek, taught herself to decipher secret messages and cipher texts.

Thanks to her good work, she managed to disrupt an important Nazi network in South America. Another important piece of her work of led directly to the imprisonment of important members of Al Capone's gang.

Main ESPIONAGE AGENCIES

In the years following World War I, each country created its own intelligence network, perfecting and developing new, increasingly complex and influential technologies. Espionage is often confused with intelligence, but they are not the same, as intelligence encompasses espionage. Intelligence services shape and transform the information obtained by spies.

SIS OR MI6
(United Kingdom, 1909—present.)

BND
(Germany, 1956—present.)

CNI
(Spain, 1935—present.)

CIA
(United States, 1947—present.)

ISI
(Pakistan, 1948—present.)

SD and GESTAPO
(Germany, 1933—1945)

FBI
(United States, 1908—present.)

MOSSAD
(Israel, 1949—present.)

KGB
(Soviet Union, 1954—1991)

PET
(Denmark, 1951—present.)

STASI
(Germany, 1950—1990)

CISEN
(Mexico, 1989—2018)

FSB
(Russia, 1995—present.)

OPERATION HIMMLER

Covert operation planned by the SS Intelligence Service that resulted in the invasion of Poland by the German army. World War II was on the cards.

CHURCHILL'S FAVORITE SPY

Maria Krystyna Janina Skarbek (1908–1952) was born in Warsaw, Poland. During the Second World War she emigrated to England and offered herself to the Special Operations Directorate, the SOE (Service Operations Executives), to fight against the Nazis. Aristocratic, a polyglot, intelligent, adventurous, somewhat stubborn, and very brave, Christine Grandville (her code name) had a life like a movie. Or almost, since Ian Fleming was inspired by her to create the character of Vesper Lynd in *Casino Royale*.

Her first mission included her parachuting over Hungary and reaching Poland to build up a network of very valuable information. Another incredible mission involved her crossing the whole of Europe in temperatures of minus 30 °C while hiding a microfilm detailing the Nazi plans to invade the Soviet Union inside her leather gloves. She made it back to England and placed the microfilm on the desk of the British Prime Minister, Winston Churchill, cementing her as his favorite spy.

GARBO, THE SPY WHO FOOLED HITLER

He was known as Garbo to the British and Arabel to the Germans, but his real name was Juan Pujol García (1912–1988). He was a rebellious student, compulsive reader, day laborer on a chicken farm, and the most important Spanish spy of all time.

He offered himself as a spy in the British embassy, but was rejected. This did not deter him, and he hatched a plan to win over the Germans in order to interest the Allies.

This master of espionage spoke neither English nor German, but his intelligence and his secret work were key. He fooled Hitler himself into believing that the Normandy landing was a diversionary maneuver; that the real Allied offensive would be at Calais. By the time the Nazis realized the deception, it was too late. In this way, Garbo saved millions of lives.

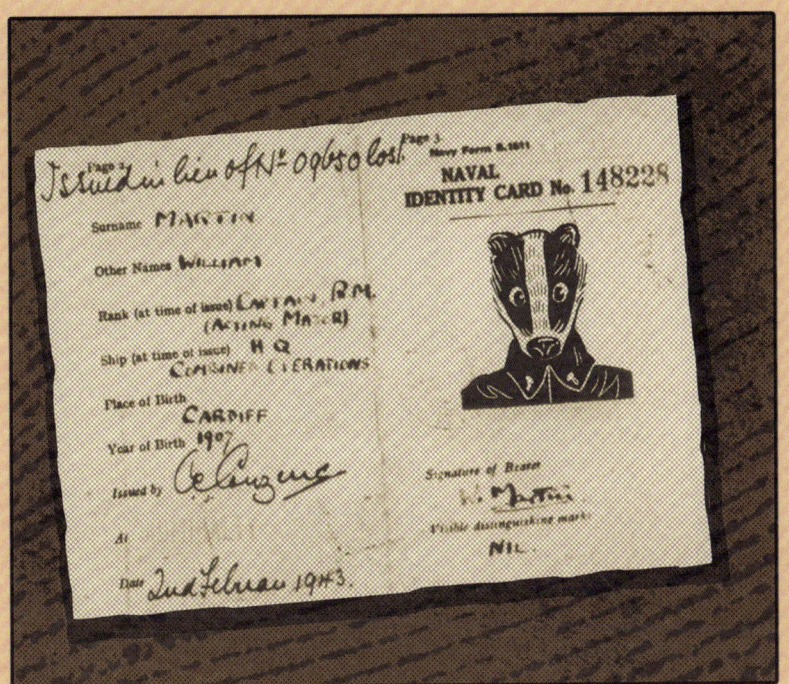

OPERATION MINCEMEAT

In 1943 a fisherman from Punta Umbria found the body of a British officer, Major William Martin, floating in the sea. He had a briefcase chained to his body with false documentation and was carrying a fake identity card, some keys, theatre tickets, and a letter to his girlfriend. This was all false documentation, created to support the character—in reality, this was a man who had died in a London hospital.

A skillful maneuver conceived and planned by the British commander Ewen Montagu, these documents provided the Germans a false exact point of the landing of the Allied forces in Europe. The Germans investigated the documents and believed everything in the briefcase. That is why they came to think that the Allies were going to land in Greece, when in fact they landed in Sicily.

THE GOLDEN AGE OF ESPIONAGE

After the end of World War II, the world was divided into two blocs: the one led by the United States and the one symbolized by the Soviet Union, which gave rise to the Cold War. There was terrible ideological, political, social, military, and even sporting confrontation. But neither bloc took direct action against the other.

Cases of espionage, double agents, treason, blackmail…these multiplied by a countless amount. If being a spy is already a high-risk profession in itself, in these delicate years it was the most dangerous job in the world—even more so than being a window cleaner on a skyscraper.

The Idealistic Traitor

Harold Adrian Russell Philby (1912—1988), better known as "Kim" (after Rudyard Kipling's novel *Kim*) Philby, is considered the most extraordinary British spy of all time. He was the highest-ranking mole in the secret service, a MI6 agent and double agent who worked for the KGB, supplying invaluable information to the Russians for 30 years before fleeing, overwhelmed by the evidence against him.

It is said that he mastered the three basic elements of espionage like no one else: betrayal, lies, and secrecy.

The Israeli Superspy

Eli Cohen (1924—1965) was an Israeli Mossad spy who called himself Kamal Amin Ta'abet. Thanks to the information he obtained on military missions, he helped Israel win the Six-Day War.

One of the events that marked his legend was the poisoned gift he gave to the Syrian army: evergreen trees with invasive roots—simple eucalyptus trees. The heat in the Syrian bunkers was suffocating and Kamal Amin gave the eucalyptus trees to provide shade. But they also served as a signal to the Israeli army.

In 1965, the Syrian special services (thanks to a special device for intercepting radio waves), raided his room and caught the spy red-handed sending a coded message. He was tried and then executed in Damascus. Mysteriously, his remains disappeared. They are still being searched for today.

Most Wanted

Nancy Wake (1912— 2011) was the most wanted spy of World War II. In occupied France, where she landed by parachute, she played a very important role in the Resistance which became a real nightmare for the Gestapo. The secret police of Nazi Germany put a very high price on her head and tortured her husband to death in an unsuccessful attempt to discover her whereabouts. She was so elusive that the Nazis nicknamed her, "the white mouse".

She was a leader, a warrior, and a fiercely independent woman. She fought against injustice and blazed a trail for modern women.

"Freedom is the only thing worth living for. While I was doing that work, I used to think that if I died, it didn't matter, because without freedom was is no point in living." Wake said in one of her best-known quotes.

The Petticoat Panel

This was a committee formed in 1953 by some CIA agents to analyze the situation of women in the agency, and determine whether they had been discriminated against on the basis of gender. This was proven to be true and they were tasked with suggesting changes to stop this happening.

EDWARD SNOWDEN

This former CIA technician did not go East or West as might have happened in the Cold War. In 2013, he simply exposed a global network of spying by the secret services on all of us. In other words: be alert.

GLOBALIZATION OF ESPIONAGE | Today's espionage capabilities are massive and indiscriminate.

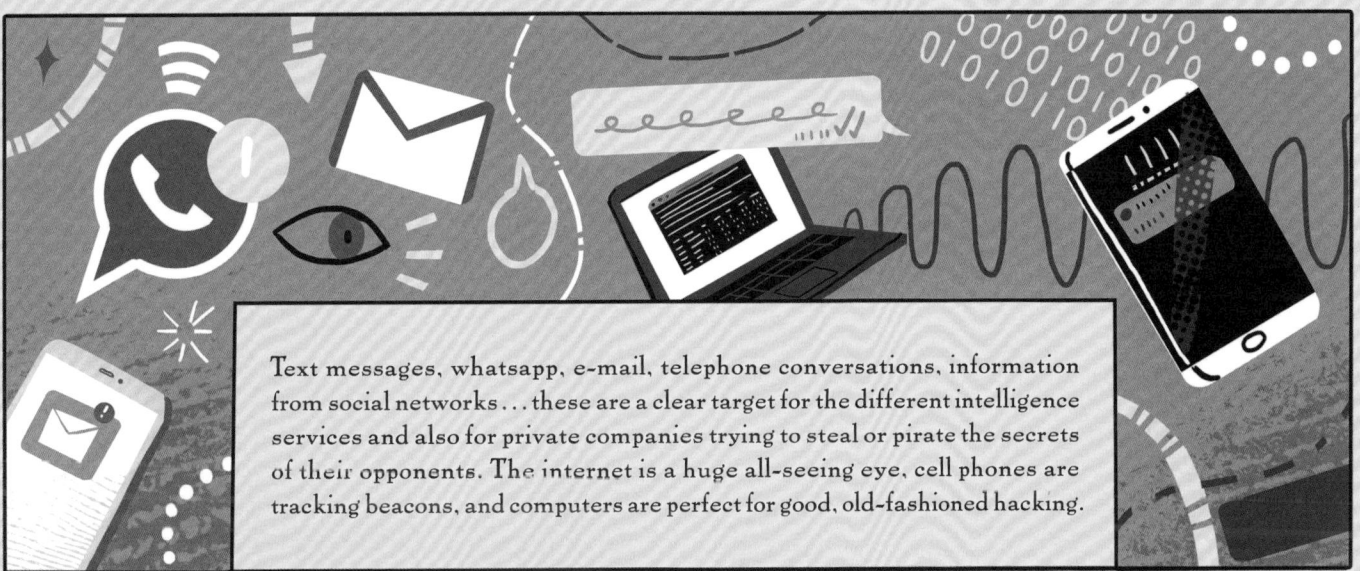

Text messages, whatsapp, e-mail, telephone conversations, information from social networks...these are a clear target for the different intelligence services and also for private companies trying to steal or pirate the secrets of their opponents. The internet is a huge all-seeing eye, cell phones are tracking beacons, and computers are perfect for good, old-fashioned hacking.

YOUR SPIES FOR MY SPIES

The summer of 2010 saw the biggest exchange of spies since the Cold War between the U.S. and Russian governments. It was at Vienna International Airport. No recordings or pictures of the event were allowed, and there was no official confirmation (or denial) that such an exchange took place. Nevertheless, the exchange of ten alleged Russian spies for four alleged members of the US secret services was reported. Among the Russian spies released were the young businesswoman, designer, and model Anna Chapman, the Peruvian journalist Vicky Pelaez, and the travel agent Mikhail Semenko. Among the spies who returned to the United States were nuclear scientist Igor Sutiaguin and military intelligence officer Sergey Skripal.

TILL THE FBI DO US PART

Elena Vavilova and her husband, Andrei Bezrukov, were recruited by the Soviet Union to work as spies. In 1999 they were posted to the United States, where they lived incognito on the outskirts of Boston. There, she lived as Tracey Foley and worked in real estate, and her husband was consultant Donald Heathfield. They were posing as Canadians. Their two children did not know the true identity of their parents, who avoided speaking Russian in front of them. A decade later they were arrested by the FBI and deported along with other agents in the most publicized spy swap since the Cold War. The series *The Americans* was inspired by the life of this unique married couple of KGB spies.

FICTIONAL SPIES

JAMES WORMOLD. A mediocre vacuum cleaner salesman and protagonist of Graham Greene's novel *Our Man in Havana*, a blend of spy novel and true-crime comedy set against the backdrop of the Cold War.

RICHARD HANNAY. He is the protagonist of *The 39 Steps*, a novel by John Buchan set in 1914 and made into a film by the fantastic Alfred Hitchcock. Richard Hannay becomes the suspect of a crime he did not commit, and this event triggers an espionage case that endangers world peace.

GEORGE SMILEY. He is the main protagonist of John Le Carré's work. He appears in the novels *Call for the Dead*, *Murder of Carla*, *The Mole*, *The Spy Who Came in from the Cold*...Smiley is a middle-aged man, short, stocky, melancholic, of vulgar appearance, and agent of the Circus. A prototypical secret agent who would never attract attention.

KIM. Kim is the child protagonist of the novel of the same title by Nobel Prize winner Rudyard Kipling. An orphan, raised on the streets of Lahore, Kim becomes the disciple of an elderly Tibetan lama whom he accompanies on a journey throughout India. A journey that is, at the same time, a secret mission in the service of British espionage.

NIKITA. She is the female icon of the spy genre. The film *Nikita* was released in 1990 and spun off into a television series. Nikita, a rootless, troubled teenager, is rescued from prison by a secret agency known as Division. After faking her execution, she is given a second chance to help her country.

JAMES BOND. He is, without a doubt, the most popular secret agent on the planet. Created by Ian Fleming, he appears for the first time in the novel *Casino Royale* (1953). The real fame of James Bond came when he made the leap to the big screen. It is believed that almost two thirds of the world's population has seen one of the films starring Agent 007.

ALEC LEAMAS. He is the protagonist of John Le Carré's *The Spy Who Came in from the Cold* (according to many, the best spy novel of all time). Leamas is a veteran British agent infiltrated in the intelligence service of the German Democratic Republic who, somewhat jaded, decides to accept the last mission that Control entrusts him.

INSPECTOR GADGET. He is the protagonist (half human, half cyborg) of a cartoon series. Despite his clumsiness, thanks to his crazy gadgets, he was able to solve dark secret cases. Dr. Claw (mysterious leader of the evil M.A.D. organization) was his number one enemy.

Daniel Nesquens

My name is Nesquens Zero Seven. You can remove the zero, even the seven, but nothing else. I am a writer. One of those who write.

Years ago, when I was still a kid, I overheard a conversation between two spies. "Send us the best possible report," said the taller one, the one with the mustache, to the shorter one, the one with glasses.

I was chasing a piece of paper that had escaped from my school folder (you know how the wind blows in Zaragoza). The sheet of paper contained the school homework that Don Máximo had given us that afternoon. "At least you have to do three of the four problems," he had told us. "Minimum or minimum?" asked my friend Gamón. "Go! Out of class, out of class," Don Máximo told him two seconds before the bell sounded. The sheet of paper got caught between the shiny boots of the tallest spy.

"What are you doing there, brat? Are you spying on us?", he blurted out.

I showed them the paper with the math problems and stared at them as only secret agents do. I didn't know what to answer. The one with glasses answered. He said:

"You have to pour twelve litres to fill the wood tank. And the distance the train will travel is eighty-eight kilometers."

I thanked him and left.

Thanks to that incident I became interested in the world of espionage. I watched…I don't know how many movies, read I don't know how many books. I painted on a mustache with a burnt cork, created my own Nesquens code, and wrote a whole notebook with those cute phrases that only good spies know how to say. "What are you doing with that, butthead?" was my favorite phrase until my father grounded me. But I had others too, like "There's not enough evidence to draw a firm conclusion." or "What's going on here?" and "We've asked for information through Interpol…"

"You have only solved two of the four problems," Don Máximo told me the next day.

"Uh…" I answered. "There is not enough evidence to draw a firm conclusion."

Oyemathias

First of all, I must tell you that this message will self-destruct in ten seconds, so I will quickly tell you a few things about myself.

My name is Mathias. There is an orange cat who really likes lasagna who has a name that sounds similar to my last name. But I always sign my name as "oyemathias", because my last name is very complex and very secret. So much so that I had to encode it in this series of letters "WMIPJIPH".

I'm sure you're in a hurry, so I'll leave you a hint: on page 25, there are some guides that may help you.

Now, enough of the riddles and let's get down to business.

I am an illustrator. One who sits at his computer with the intention of drawing, but who is often on his balcony looking at the little dogs that pass under his house.

I love to go to city parks to think up ideas for drawings and crazy projects that I then write down in my notebook (although because of my bad handwriting, neither I, nor the best spy can decipher them later).

I come from a country called Chile, which is narrow and long. Did you know that in other places they call chili a pepper that makes your tongue burn when you eat it?

Well, in Mexico they eat my country with meat.

That's all for now; as a reward for finishing the whole book, I've cancelled the destruction of this message. You are welcome.